Instant Scroll Saw Projects

Instant Scroll Saw Projects

Patrick Spielman

Sterling Publishing Co. Inc., New York

A Sterling/Chapelle Book

Chapelle Ltd.

Owner:
Jo Packham

Design/Layout Editor:
Gerry De Soto

Staff:
Marie Barber, Ann Bear, Areta Bingham, Kass Burchett, Rebecca Christensen, Holly Fuller, Marilyn Goff, Shirley Heslop, Holly Hollingsworth, Shawn Hsu, Susan Jorgensen, Pauline Locke, Barbara Milburn, Linda Orton, Karmen Quinney, Rhonda Rainey, Leslie Ridenour, and Cindy Stoeckl.

Photography:
Kevin Dilley, photographer for Hazen Photography

Photo Stylist:
Leslie Liechty

Library of Congress Cataloging-in-Publication Data

Spielman, Patrick E.
    Instant scroll saw projects / Patrick Spielman.
        p.   cm.
    "A Sterling/Chapelle book."
    Includes index.
    ISBN 0-8069-8641-7
    1. Jig saws. 2. Woodwork--Patterns.   I. Title.
TT186.S6655   1998
745.51'3--dc21   98-3574
                                    CIP

A Sterling/Chapelle Book

Published by Sterling Publishing Company, Inc.
387 Park Avenue South, New York, NY 10016
© 1998 by Chapelle Ltd.
Distributed in Canada by Sterling Publishing
c/o Canadian Manda Group,
One Atlantic Avenue, Suite 105
Toronto, Ontario, Canada M6K 3E7
Distributed in Great Britain and Europe by Cassell PLC
Wellington House, 125 Strand,
London WC2R 0BB, England
Distributed in Australia by Capricorn Link
(Australia) Pty Ltd.
P.O. Box 6651, Baulkham Hills, Business Centre, NSW
2153, Australia
Printed in China
All Rights Reserved

Sterling ISBN 0-8069-8641-7

Every effort has been made to ensure that all of the information in this book is accurate. However, due to differing conditions, tools, and individual skills, the publisher cannot be responsible for any injuries, losses, and/or other damages which may result from the use of the information in this book.

If you have any questions or comments or would like information about any specialty products featured in this book, please contact:

Chapelle Ltd., Inc.
P.O. Box 9252
Ogden, UT 84409

Phone: (801) 621-2777
FAX: (801) 621-2788

Table of Contents:

Project Gallery:

Instant Scroll Saw Projects

Instant Scroll Saw Projects is intended for those who want to make decorative scroll saw projects easily and quickly. This is a book for people of every age who enjoy cutting figures from wood, but, like many of us, simply lack the confidence, skill, or time to artistically paint on the necessary details to fully complete the project.

Essentially, all you need to do is permanently adhere a color copy of the prepared artwork pattern to a piece of wood that is approximately the same shape and size and cut out the piece(s) with your scroll saw. Since the artwork is prepainted for you, you do not need to purchase a full palette of colors nor require the expertise to use them. This is certainly a technique that guarantees success. It is fast, fun, and saves so much time that I dubbed this technique "Instant Projects."

For those new to the craft of woodworking and scroll sawing, I have included some basic information to help you get started. You will learn some fundamentals about selecting wood, how scroll saws work, features of a few popular scroll saws, and some essential techniques for using a scroll saw to make the projects in this book.

Wood Materials

To get the most from woodworking and to be successful with the scroll saw, you must select the kind of wood material that is the most practical choice for your projects.

There are good reasons why certain kinds of wood are used to make a baseball bat or a cutting board. These are hard, tough woods with properties that can withstand abuse. While good for rough usage, the same woods are not necessarily best for decorative cutouts.

In fact, these and some other woods and certain wood sheet products, if used, are certain to discourage and frustrate beginning wood workers. *See Photo No. 1.*

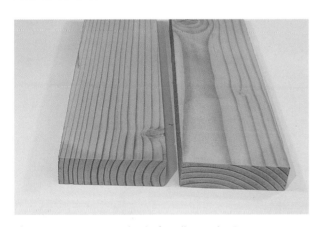

Photo No. 1. A general rule for all woods: Quarter-sawn boards, like the one on the left, will stay flatter and distort less than the plain-sawn boards on the right.

Certain woods have unfavorable qualities: weakness, cracks, splits, distorts (warps), swells, shrinks, burns, or decays. They can be too hard; too soft; too heavy; too light; not readily available; too expensive; and difficult to cut, smooth, or finish.

Wood is also categorized as hardwood or softwood. It is usually selected for specific uses, according to its physical hardness. Some of the commonly available hardwoods are: maple, ash, cherry, oak, birch, and beech. Softwoods include pine, basswood, cedar, redwood, and butternut. Mahogany, walnut, and poplar might be considered as medium-hard woods.

Solid woods most practical for making some of the simple cutouts in this book include No. 2 shop pine, poplar, and basswood. *See Photo No. 2.*

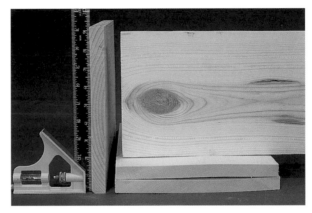

Photo No. 2. Inexpensive No. 2 shop pine is a good choice for small projects that can be cut out around defects. Sometimes boards can be found flat like the one on the left, but usually wide plain-sawn boards will have some distortion and cupping, like the boards at the lower right. Note the typical knot and pitch pockets, which are areas that should be avoided.

By purchasing less costly lower grades, you can afford to cut small projects from clear areas between defects in the wood, such as knots and pitch pockets. Discolored boards are fine, as long as there is no decay, because the surfaces will be hidden away when the color copy is adhered. Beautiful, expensive woods, like walnut and mahogany, are impractical choices because their stunning colors and figure would be hidden. As a general rule, avoid firs and cedars.

They splinter easily and produce irregular surfaces when sanded. Also, do not use pressure treated yellow or southern pine. These woods are best used outdoors for outside products and can also produce dangerous fumes and sawdust.

Plywood and Sheet Materials

Plywood and some sheet materials offer certain advantages over solid boards. They do not check or crack. They stay flat, are strong in all directions, do not swell or shrink, and are available in larger sizes. Generally, they also have uniform surface characteristics with minimal waste. However, as a rule, sheet materials manufactured for building construction should not be used for scroll saw projects. *See Photo No. 3.*

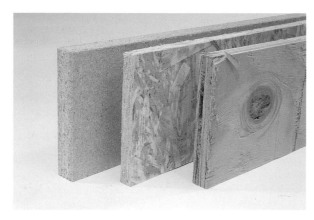

Photo No. 3. Unfavorable sheet materials for scroll sawing. Left: Particle board has hard, abrasive resins, Center: Chipboard has abrasive resins and poor surfaces, Right: Construction grade plywoods have interior voids, poor surface qualities, and splinter easily.

Some sheet materials are less expensive than solid woods; but others such as fine, hardwood plywoods, can be extremely expensive. Thinner sheets of Baltic birch and poplar plywoods are widely used by scroll saw crafts people. *See Photo No. 4.*

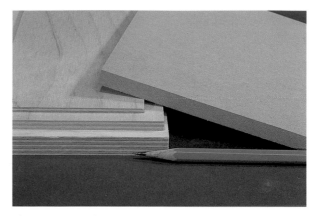

Photo No. 4. Left: Poplar plywoods and Baltic birch plywoods, in thinner sheets, are good for scroll sawing because of their void-free interiors and smooth surfaces. Baltic birch plywood thicker than 3/8" may cause blade dulling problems because of the abrasiveness of all the glue. Right: piece of MDF (medium density fiberboard).

MDF (medium density fiberboard) is not commonly used, but it is a good choice if you can obtain it. Your building products supplier may order a 4' X 8' sheet for you or maybe you can obtain scraps from a local cabinet maker. MDF is fairly inexpensive. It costs about half the price of No. 2 shop pine. It may be a bit harder on saw blades and it also generates fine dust when cut, so always wear a dust mask. MDF is manufactured from lumbering leftovers of sawdust and chips.

Scroll Saws

Scroll saws are tremendously popular woodworking machines. When compared to all other power driven devices that cut wood, the scroll saw is unquestionably the safest, the most user-friendly, and the easiest to master. Scroll sawing is enjoyed by crafters of all ages. It requires no mechanical skills and it allows you to safely cut small pieces of wood to make a variety of projects, quickly.

The major function of the scroll saw

is to cut irregular curves and openings in flat wood. A very small, narrow blade is held taut between the ends of two horizontal arms that move in unison up and down to create a reciprocating cutting motion. *See Photos No. 5 and 6.*

Photo No. 6. Blades are clamped at each end to the upper arm, and to the lower arm under the table. An important feature of scroll saw usage is its capacity for installing and changing blades quickly and easily.

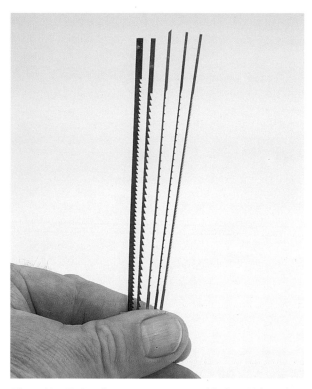

Photo No. 5. Scroll saws carry narrow blades. Although narrower blades than these are available, you will not need any finer than these. A general rule: Use wider blades with fewer teeth for sawing larger curves and cutting thicker woods; use narrower blades with more teeth for intricate details in thin woods.

The blade moves vertically through an opening in the saw table. The operator supports the work piece on the table and advances it into the blade in a manner that is similar to feeding fabric under the needle of a sewing machine.

Because the very narrow blades are extremely sharp, arcs and turns can be cut to make highly detailed and intricate objects. *See Photo No. 7.*

Scroll saws are available in a wide variety of prices, ranging from less than $100.00 to over $2,000.00, with a growing list of features and options that improve the overall performance of the machine. Most projects in this book can be made using any scroll saw, including the least expensive. There are many brands to choose from and some manufacturers offer several models. Before purchasing any scroll saw, you should seriously consider the full range of work that you might want to do in the future. Scroll saws can cut a wide variety of materials,

Photo No. 7. Typical scroll saw work is cutting fine details. Thin plywood is selected for strength and the narrow blade permits cutting intricate, delicate designs with inside openings.

including various metals and plastics. Some scroll saws have more capability and capacity to saw thicker and larger sizes of wood than do others. Thus, if you want to do more than just simple cutouts, you need to investigate and try various saws, if possible, to see which saw best matches your long-term needs. For a more advanced description of scroll saw usage and features, I recommend my previously published Sterling books *Scroll Saw Basics* and the *Scroll Saw Handbook*.

The size of the saw is designated by its "throat capacity." This is the distance from the blade to the rear of the machine. A 15" saw, for example, can cut to the center of a 30"-diameter circle. Saw sizes range from 13" to 30" and are available in bench and floor model versions. The rate at which the blade moves up and down in strokes per minute is called the "blade speed." The least expensive saws have just one constant speed. Two-speed and variable-speed saws give you better control when cutting thin or soft materials, as well as the ability to efficiently cut metal and plastic. The photos included here give you a good overview of some popular brands of saws currently available. *See Photos No. 8 through 13.*

In addition to considering variable-speed saws, some saw features worth considering are up-front controls, i.e.: blade tensioning, on-off switch, and blade speed adjustment. Look into adaptability, i.e.: adding a light, a magnifier, dust collection, and/or blower. A foot switch is a good optional accessory. Remember, the most important feature to look for is its capacity for changing blades quickly and/or threading the blade through the work piece easily for making inside cuts.

Photo No. 8. A Sears Craftsman 16" variable-speed, bench-top scroll saw. Costs about $200.00.

Photo No. 9. A Royobi 16 " scroll saw will cut stock up to 2" in thickness and features a shop-vac connection port for dust removal. Costs about $175.00.

Photo No. 10. Delta's two-speed 16" scroll saw is one of several models available from the manufacturer. Costs about $175.00.

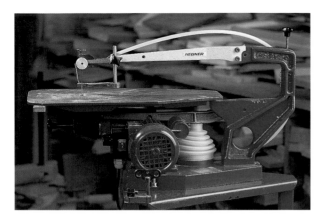

Photo No. 11. Hegner's 18" variable-speed features up-front tensioning. Costs about $1000.00.

Photo No. 12. De Walt's 20" variable-speed saw is one of the newest brands available with many innovative features. Costs about $475.00.

Photo No. 13. Excalibur's 30" variable-speed has the largest throat capacity available. Costs about $1400.00.

Blades

Blades are fairly inexpensive, costing between 20¢ to 75¢ each, depending upon size, style, quantity, and quality. The most popular blade is the 5" plain-end type. Sizes are designated by numbers and range from Nos. 2/0 and 0 in very fine, to Nos. 1, 2, and 4 in fine, to Nos. 5 to 7 in medium, and Nos. 8 to 12 in large sizes. Photo No. 5 on page 9 illustrates some medium and fine sizes. Medium blades are recommended for completing the projects in this book.

There are various blade tooth design configurations available, with skip tooth being one of the most popular. *See Drawing No. 1.*

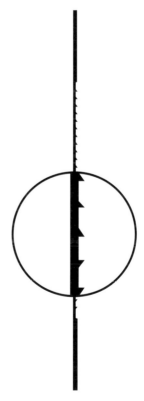

Drawing No. 1. Skip tooth design with reversed lower teeth minimizes bottom splintering or feathering along the cut edges of the piece.

This blade tooth design provides for fast sawdust removal and consequently provides cooler and smoother cuts. The skip tooth design is exactly as stated – every other tooth is eliminated. Another popular design is the double skip tooth blade, which has two adjoining teeth following a skip. Look for blades with reversed lower teeth. These minimize tear-out or splintering as the teeth exit the bottom of the work piece.

The best, newest, and most expensive blades are ground from tempered steel with abrasive wheels. These are known as "ground blades." They last longer and cut straighter when compared to less expensive milled or stamped blades that have burr edges along the sides. *See Drawing No. 2.* The burr edge is the result of material flow during manufacturing. The burr-edge side of the blade is sharper and provides less cutting resistance than the non-burr side of the blade. This causes the blade to track slightly to one side while cutting – a condition for which you will learn to compensate. The side-tracking tendency of these blades is especially noticeable when making straight line cuts.

For general softwood cutting, use the larger blades, Nos. 7 to 12 for 3/4" and thicker stock. Use Nos. 5 to 7 for 1/2" to 3/4" stock, and Nos. 1 to 5 for 1/8" to 1/2" stock. I recommend just three blades: No. 4, No. 7, and No. 9. These will handle most of the cutting projects in this book.

Avoid spiral blades. Although designed to cut efficiently in all directions, they are not a good choice for beginners. They cut slowly and leave a very rough-sawn surface.

Use ground blades for the smoothest-sawn surfaces. They stay sharp longer when cutting plywoods and also make smooth cuts in pine.

The slight front to back movement of the blade during the cutting stroke of the scroll saw produces a sawn surface that is smooth and seldom needs sanding.

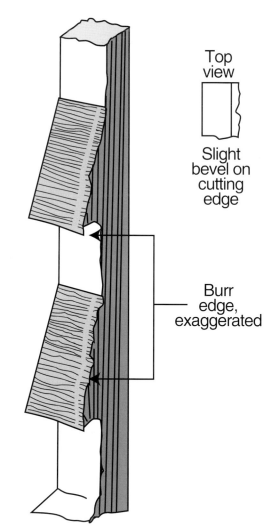

Top view

Slight bevel on cutting edge

Burr edge, exaggerated

Drawing No. 2. This enlarged sketch shows the sharp, microscopic metal burr along one edge of the blade. This condition is typical of less expensive scroll saw blades. It is caused by the way blades are manufactured. For this reason, scroll saw blades actually track unevenly, because there is more cutting resistance on one edge of the blade than the other.

The Basic Techniques

It is important to touch upon some fundamentals that pertain to preparation, basic sawing skills, special techniques for clock inserts, and final finishing of the project(s).

Preparation

Make certain to first read and review the owner's manual and observe all of the safety precautions relative to the use of the scroll saw. For most of the projects, you'll need to make cuts with the saw table set square to the blade. Use a small square or a protractor to make and check this adjustment. The factory calibrations on the blade-tilt scales of most scroll saws are difficult to read (especially with bifocals) and most are not accurate. *See Photo No. 14.*

Photo No. 14. Using a simple protractor as shown, is the easiest way to check the squareness of the table to the blade and to adjust table tilt to the desired angle for bevel cutting.

Make certain that you have the blade installed with the teeth pointing downward. Tension it correctly, according to the manufacturer's instructions. If you have never cut before, I recommend making some preliminary cuts until you gain confidence and can follow various lines consistently. The most difficult types of cuts to make accurately are: perfectly straight lines; a true radius or full circle; and other geometric shapes, such as ovals, squares, and any parallel lines that run close together. *See Photo No. 15.* Patience and practice are the keys to developing sawing skills.

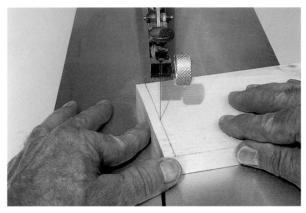

Photo No. 15. Practice straight-line cutting parallel to an edge. The work is guided against the left forefinger. The feed direction here appears to be somewhat angular, and it actually is. This is because of the type of blade being used. It has a burr edge on the right side of the blade, resulting from the blade manufacturing process. Ground blades are uniformly sharp on both sides of the blade and do not require this compensation adjustment in feed directions.

Artwork Preparation

Determine if you want to use the artwork at the size provided in the book. Each piece of art can be color-copied to any size you choose. Sometimes a slight adjustment in size will allow you to make full use of a piece of wood. A slight size reduction may allow you to fit the artwork onto a piece of wood that you may otherwise have discarded.

A proportion scale can help you determine the exact percentage of reduction or enlargement required before making a color copy of the artwork for your project. *See Photo No. 16 on page 14.*

Quality color copies can be made at any retail copy establishment for a minimal fee. Ask the copy attendant to match the colors as closely as possible and to help with the reduction and enlargements, if necessary.

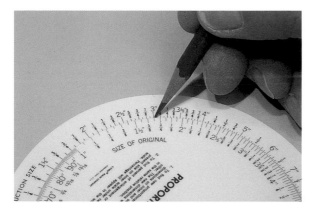

Photo No. 16. A proportion scale is used to determine optimum sizes when reducing or enlarging artwork on copy machines. Simply align the mark indicating the existing size of the artwork in the book, then turn the scale to the desired finished size and take note of the percentage in the window. Set the copy machine to the percentage as designated in the proportion scale's window.

Using scissors, cut the excess paper from around the color copy, leaving about 1/2" beyond the shape of the design. The wood should be slightly larger than the copy. *See Photos No. 17, 18, and 19.*

There are two different methods for adhering the color copy to the wood, using either 3M's Photo Mount® or decoupage medium.

Spray Adhesive Method

Spray the back of the cut out color copy with the adhesive and apply it to the wood. Using your fingers or rubber roller, start at the center and work toward outside edges, flattening any air bubbles. The spray adhesive does not require an extensive drying time. Follow manufacturer's instructions. *See Photos No. 17 and 18.*

Photo No. 17. Using scissors, cut the excess paper from around the color copy, leaving about 1/2" beyond the shape of the design.

Photo No. 18. This color copy is adhered to the wood with 3M's Photo Mount® spray adhesive. *See Photo No. 17.*

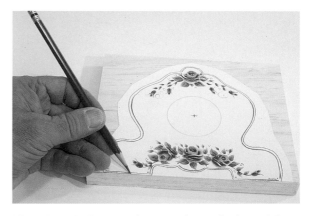

Photo No. 19. Some projects require perfectly straight edges, such as the bottom of this clock. Rather than trying to cut a straight line with the scroll saw, adhere the edge of the color copy to the factory-cut straight edge of the wood.

Decoupage Method

Using a large, flat brush, apply a generous coat of decoupage medium to the wood. Quickly press the cut color copy into the wet medium. Using your fingers or a rubber roller, start at the center and work toward outside edges, flattening any air bubbles. Set aside and let dry thoroughly. *See Photos No. 20A, 20B, and 20C.*

Apply two coats of decoupage medium over the color copy, allowing the coats to dry between applications. *See Photo No. 20D.* Let the wood dry for at least an hour, or until the color copy is no longer cool to the touch. Once the piece is completely dry, it is ready to be cut out with the scroll saw.

Photo No. 20A. Cut out a piece of wood that is roughly the size and shape of the color copy of artwork.

Photo No. 20C. Using fingers or a rubber roller, gently rub out any bubbles or folds in the color copy. Work from the middle out to the edges of the color copy.

Photo No. 20B. Apply a generous coat of decoupage medium onto the wood. Quickly press color copy into wet medium.

Photo No. 20D. Apply two coats of the decoupage medium over the color copy, letting the coats dry between each application. Let the work piece dry until it is no longer cool to the touch.

Tips for Thin Work Pieces

Plywoods that are 1/4" and thinner, are not easy to cut unless you have a slow-speed saw. Even with a slow-speed saw, always use a waste-backer nailed, glued, or double-sided taped under the work piece. *See Photo No. 21.* A waste-backer adds "blade resistance," giving you better sawing control. The waste-backer also minimizes tearout and splintering on the bottom of the work piece. Used plywood or paneling makes an effective, yet inexpensive waste-backer material.

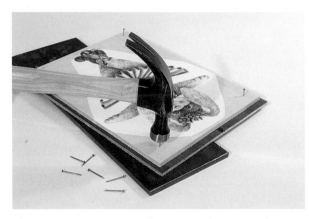

Photo No. 21. Preparation for cutting thin material. A waste-backer is secured under the work piece. Small brads are driven through both pieces while held over a flat piece of metal. The metal peens the nails on the bottom side. This technique works well with plywoods, even as thin as 1/32" thick.

Basic Sawing Tips

Beginners should use the hold-down and guard. *See Photo No. 22.* Making sharp "on-the-spot" turns to cut inside corners and acute angles requires some practice and a fairly narrow blade. There are alternative techniques for successfully making these cuts. *See Photos No. 23, 24, and 26.*

Some projects have inside openings that may be cut away. Simply drill small holes in the waste area and thread

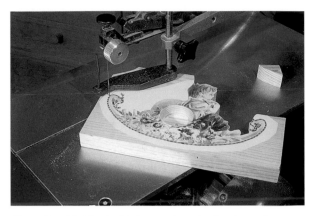

Photo No. 22. The hold-down gives the beginner better control, especially when making sharp turns. Inside cut-outs are made and a recessed opening for a clock insert is completed before cutting the outside profile.

the blade through the work piece, then reattach it to your saw and begin cutting. *See Photos No. 25 and 26.*

With most projects, the artwork provides cutting lines to follow. It does not matter if you cut directly on the line or slightly on the inside of it. If you cut too far outside the line, it remains and needs to be sanded away later. Some pieces of artwork do not have distinct cutting lines. In most cases, the scroll saw will make a cut so smooth that no sanding is required unless you need to sand to improve the size or shape of the work piece.

Photo No. 23. Beginners, using wide blades, may be more comfortable rounding sharp inside cuts like this, then completing the cut later by making an inward cut from the opposite direction.

Photo No. 24. Completing the inside corner cut. *See Photo No. 23.*

Photo No. 25. Threading the blade to cut out an inside opening. Note the four holes drilled around the face.

Photo No. 26. Cutting out an inside opening. A series of short cuts into the corner widens the blade path (kerf), permitting the work piece to be turned without twisting the blade.

Preparation for Clock Inserts

Clock inserts require very accurate round holes or recesses. The popular mini-clocks have an outside diameter that is about 1 7/16" and require an exact 1 3/8"-diameter hole, leaving little room for error. It is best to simply bore a hole, using a 1 3/8" multi-spur bit. *See Photo No. 27.*

Photo No. 27. A 1 3/8" multi-spur bit makes the correct size hole for a mini-clock insert. Make a small starting hole with a drill bit when cutting the hole opening.

If you don't have the correct size bit, you can cut and sand the hole opening by hand or with a drum sander to fit. *See Photo No. 28.*

Photo No. 28. Creating an opening for a clock insert requires an accurate layout line and careful cutting. It is best to cut to the inside of the line and then sand out to the layout line.

The hole diameter should be perfectly sized, so just the friction of the insert against the sides of the hole holds the clock in place.

Edge Work and Finishing

Remember, when sanding edges, stroke just toward the color copy and against the wood so you do not flake off the edges or lift it from the bond. If you elect to finish the edges, simply paint them and the back with acrylics in coordinating colors. *See Photo No. 29.* When complete, dry spray the project with a matte or gloss top-coat of a vinyl or polyurethane finish. Add any further embellishments such as bells, raffia, or whatever pleases your interest and eye.

Photo No. 29. Using a small brush, paint the sawn edges, brushing from the center toward the outside edge.

Safety

The use and understanding of any power tool contribute to the success and sense of accomplishment that come with a job well done. The materials used by a crafts person can be dangerous and potentially lethal. The combination of potentially noxious dust, harmful chemicals and paints, high noise levels, sharp tools, and high quantities of electricity make it imperative that the crafts person operates a safe, clean, and well thought-out environment. The risk of injury should never be underestimated.

Remember the following safety guidelines:

• Understand and observe strict rules with regard to manufacturer's instructions in the safe operation of all tools.

• Always wear a respirator or dust mask while working.

• Wear eye and ear protection when working with power tools.

• Never allow fingers to come near any moving blades or cutters.

• Wear appropriate attire – a heavy work apron, no jewelry, and no loose sleeves or ties. Wear appropriate footwear to protect feet from sharp or dropped objects.

• Feel comfortable when using power tools. Think out your project in its entirety and understand all aspects of it before beginning.

• Always keep your mind on your work. Do not allow your mind to wander or be distracted when using power tools or sharp objects. Above all, never work when tired, in a hurry, or not in the mood. Put the project down for today and come back to it later, in a better frame of mind and with time to spare.

• Use common sense at all times and you will enjoy each and every new challenging project and idea.

Basic Project Supplies
required to create
the projects within this book:

Color copy of project artwork

Scissors

3M Photo Mount® or decoupage medium

Rubber roller

Scroll saw

Drill and 1/16", 1/8", 1/4", forstner,
and multi-spur bits

Pencil

Sandpaper

Paint brushes

Lady Plant Stick

Materials:
1/4" Baltic birch plywood
1/4" dowel 14" long
All purpose glue
Paint (coordinated colors)

Instructions:
Adhere color copy to plywood. Cut out design.
Glue one end of dowel to back of work piece.
Paint back and edges of the work piece. Paint
the dowel.

21

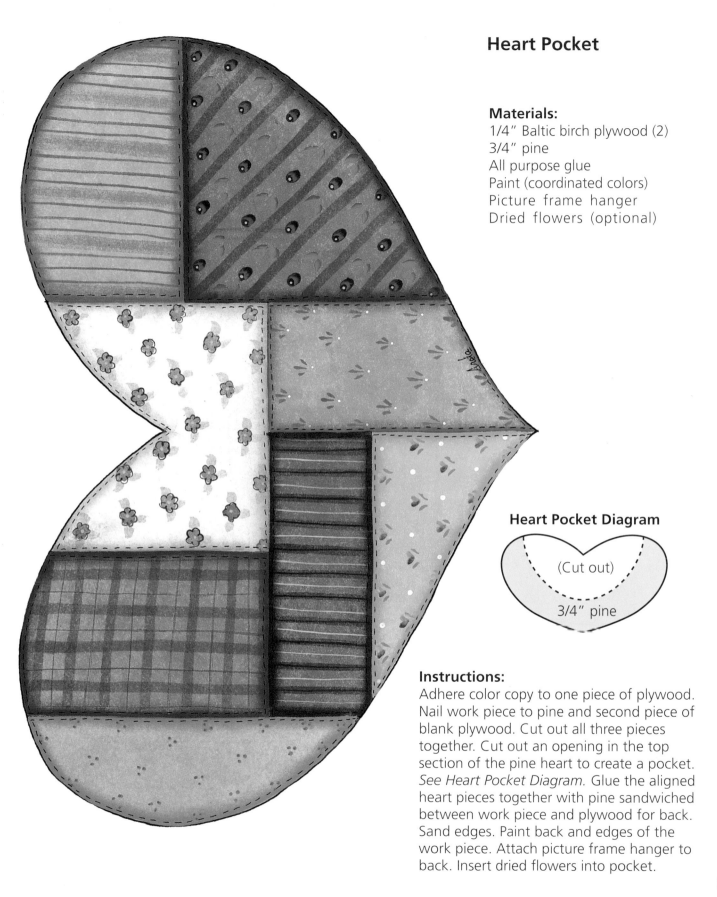

Heart Pocket

Materials:
1/4" Baltic birch plywood (2)
3/4" pine
All purpose glue
Paint (coordinated colors)
Picture frame hanger
Dried flowers (optional)

Heart Pocket Diagram

(Cut out)

3/4" pine

Instructions:
Adhere color copy to one piece of plywood.
Nail work piece to pine and second piece of
blank plywood. Cut out all three pieces
together. Cut out an opening in the top
section of the pine heart to create a pocket.
See Heart Pocket Diagram. Glue the aligned
heart pieces together with pine sandwiched
between work piece and plywood for back.
Sand edges. Paint back and edges of the
work piece. Attach picture frame hanger to
back. Insert dried flowers into pocket.

ABCDEFGHIJKLMNOPQRSTUVWXYZ
ABCDEFGHIJKLMNOPQRSTUVWXYZ
ABCDEFGHIJKLMNOPQRSTUVWXYZ
ABCDEFGHIJKLMNOPQRSTUVWXYZ
English
Spelling
A-Z

A Teacher's Frame

(Cut out)

Note: When making a color copy of the frame artwork, reduce or enlarge to match photograph size.

Materials:
1/4" Baltic birch plywood
All purpose glue
Paint (coordinated colors)
Mat or tag board for backing

Instructions:
Adhere color copy to plywood. Cut out design. Cut out mat or tag board to frame size for a backing for the frame. Paint edges of work piece. Glue only the bottom and the right side of the mat or tag board to the back of the frame, leaving the other two sides open for the insertion of photograph.

Bear Hearts Umbrella

Materials:
3/4" wood of choice
Paint (coordinated colors)
Picture frame hanger
Brass hook

Instructions:
Adhere color copy to wood. Cut out design. Paint back and edges of the work piece. Attach picture frame hanger to back. Screw in brass hook at the base of the umbrella handle in the artwork.

Spring Bunny

Materials:
3/4" pine
1/8" Baltic birch plywood
1/4" dowel 7 1/2" long
All purpose glue
Paint (coordinated colors)
Wire, 24 gauge
Raffia (optional)

Instructions:
Adhere color copies for bunny body, planter, basket, birdhouse, and flower pot to pine. Cut out designs. Drill 1/4" hole, 1/2" deep in bottom of birdhouse and glue in one end of dowel. Adhere color copies for bunny arms, ribbon, and sign to plywood. Cut out designs. Glue arms and ribbon to bunny. *See photo on opposite page.* Drill 1/16" holes through each corner of the sign and attach wire. Glue wire with sign under the hand of the bunny. Cut out a 3/4" X 2 3/4" X 10" base from pine. Paint base as desired. Paint backs and edges of work pieces. Arrange and glue work pieces onto the base. Drill 1/4" hole, 1/2" deep into base. Glue remaining end of dowel in base. Tie raffia bow around dowel (optional).

Baseball Bears

Materials:
1/8" Baltic birch plywood
All purpose glue
Paint (coordinated colors)
Shelf, purchased or refer to
 Materials and Instructions
 for shelf assembly on page 32
Picture frame hangers (2)

Instructions:
Adhere color copy to plywood. Cut out design. Paint edges and back of work piece. Paint purchased or assembled shelf. Glue work piece to shelf. *See photo on opposite page.* Attach picture frame hangers to back of each side of the work piece.

Materials for shelf assembly :

1/2" pine (back plate and shelf)
1/4" pine (pickets – 9, rails – 2)
Wooden pegs (4)
All purpose glue
Paint (coordinated colors)

Instructions for shelf assembly:

•Cut out nine pickets and two rails from the 1/4" pine. *See Shelf Diagrams 1 and 3.*

•Cut out backplate and shelf from 1/2" pine. *See Shelf Diagrams 2 and 3.* Drill four holes into the backplate to accommodate wooden pegs. Glue in wooden pegs.

•Evenly space pickets and glue them to the rails. *See Shelf Diagrams 1 and 4.*

•Glue bottom edge of lower rail to the top of the shelf. Glue top of backplate to the bottom of the shelf.

Shelf Diagram 1

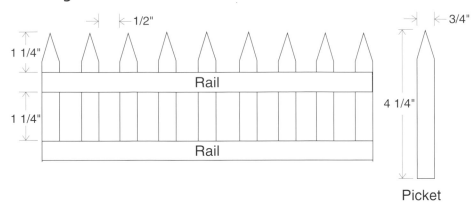

Picket

Shelf Diagram 2

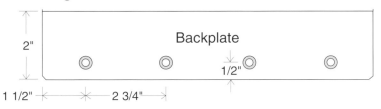

Shelf Diagram 3

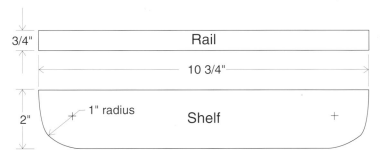

Shelf Diagram 4

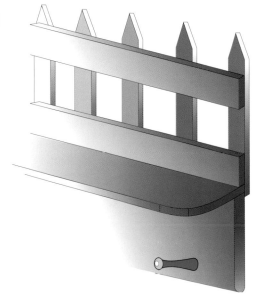

Ballerina Bunny

Materials:
1/4" Baltic birch plywood
Plaque, purchased or refer to
   Materials and Instructions
   for plaque assembly on page 35
All purpose glue
Paint (coordinated colors)
Picture frame hangers (2)

Instructions:
Adhere color copy to plywood.
Cut out design. Paint back and
edges of work piece. Paint
plaque. Attach picture frame
hangers on back of plaque.
Center and glue work piece to
plaque. *See photo on page 33.*

Materials for plaque assembly :
3/8″ pine
Wooden pegs (2)
All purpose glue
Paint (coordinated colors)

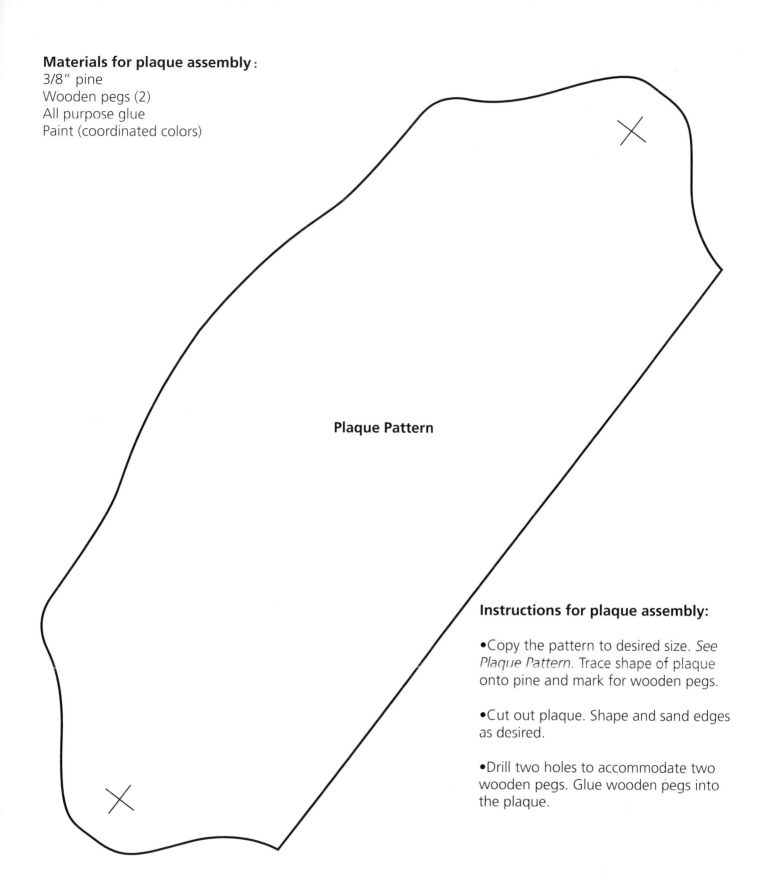

Plaque Pattern

Instructions for plaque assembly:

•Copy the pattern to desired size. *See Plaque Pattern.* Trace shape of plaque onto pine and mark for wooden pegs.

•Cut out plaque. Shape and sand edges as desired.

•Drill two holes to accommodate two wooden pegs. Glue wooden pegs into the plaque.

Chocolate Bear

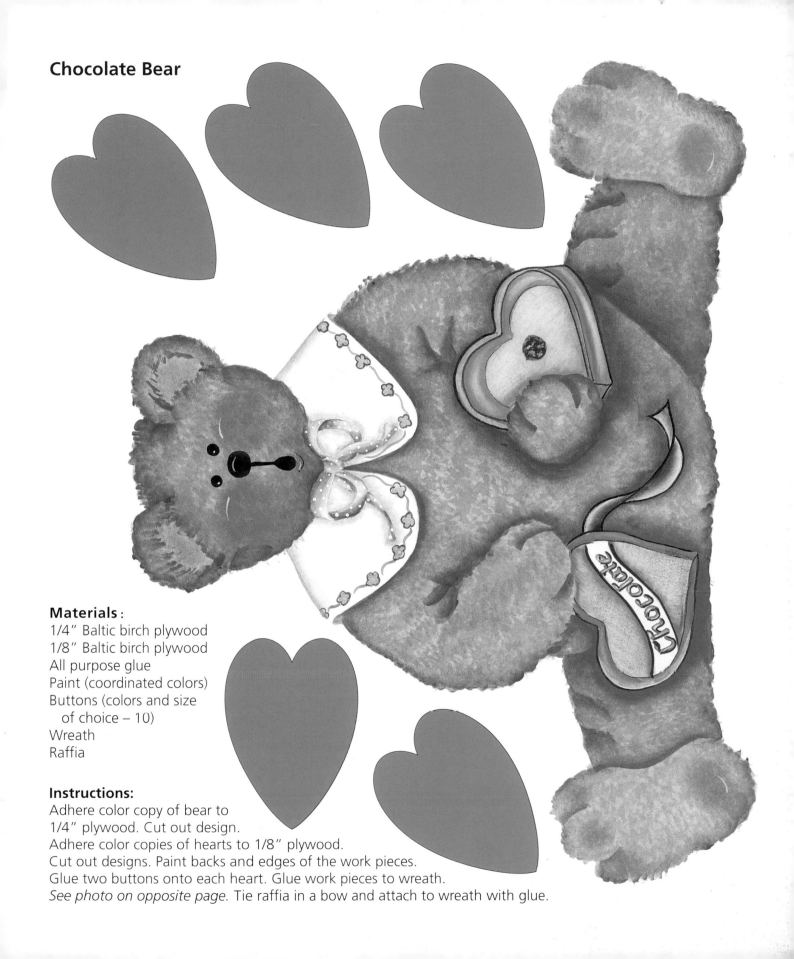

Materials:
1/4" Baltic birch plywood
1/8" Baltic birch plywood
All purpose glue
Paint (coordinated colors)
Buttons (colors and size
  of choice – 10)
Wreath
Raffia

Instructions:
Adhere color copy of bear to
1/4" plywood. Cut out design.
Adhere color copies of hearts to 1/8" plywood.
Cut out designs. Paint backs and edges of the work pieces.
Glue two buttons onto each heart. Glue work pieces to wreath.
See photo on opposite page. Tie raffia in a bow and attach to wreath with glue.

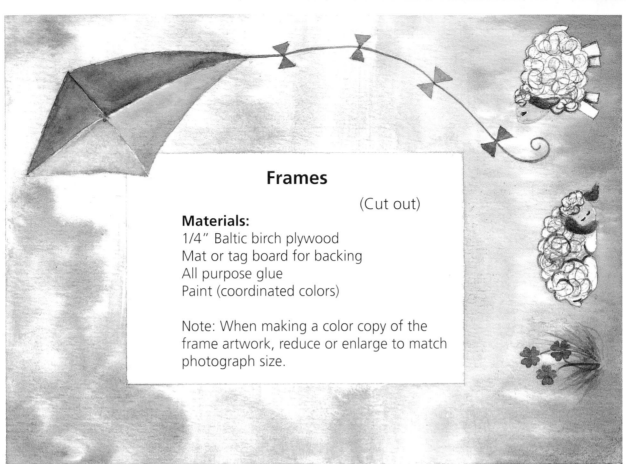

Frames

(Cut out)

Materials:
1/4" Baltic birch plywood
Mat or tag board for backing
All purpose glue
Paint (coordinated colors)

Note: When making a color copy of the frame artwork, reduce or enlarge to match photograph size.

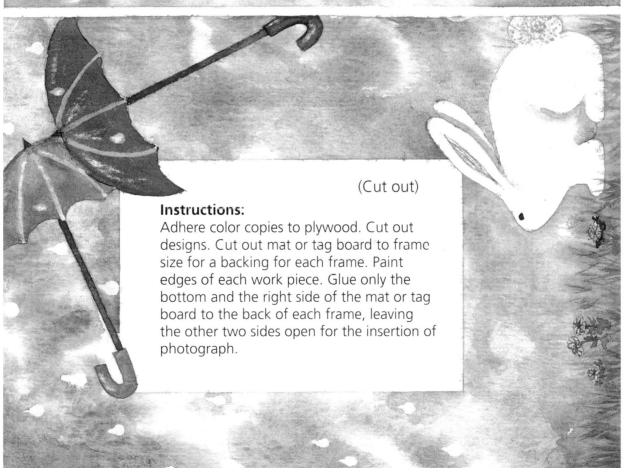

(Cut out)

Instructions:
Adhere color copies to plywood. Cut out designs. Cut out mat or tag board to frame size for a backing for each frame. Paint edges of each work piece. Glue only the bottom and the right side of the mat or tag board to the back of each frame, leaving the other two sides open for the insertion of photograph.

39

(Cut out)

(Cut out)

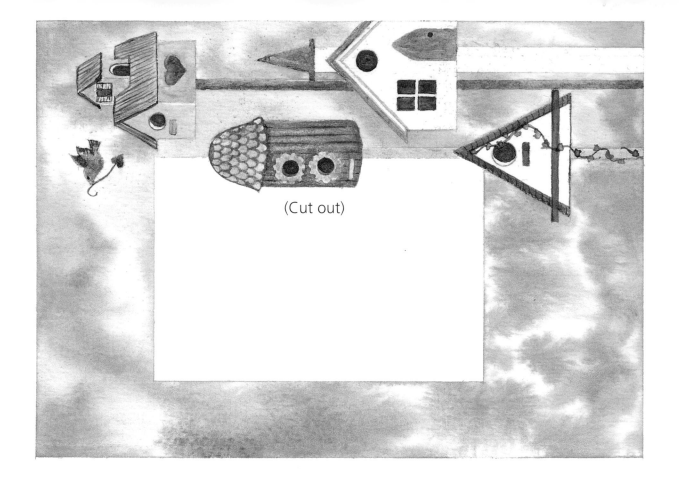

(Cut out)

(Cut out)

Birdhouses on Poles

Materials:
3/4" pine
1/4" dowel 14" long (3)
All purpose glue
Paint (coordinated colors)

Instructions:
Adhere color copies to pine. Cut out designs. Drill 1/4" hole, 1/2" deep into bottom of each work piece. Glue dowels in work pieces. Paint the back and edges of the work pieces and dowels.

Birdhouse Candle Holders

Materials:
1 1/2" wood of choice
Paint (coordinated colors)
Candles of choice

Instructions:
Adhere color copies to wood. Cut out designs. Drill holes 1" deep into the top of each work piece to accommodate candles. Paint the backs and edges of the work pieces.

45

2 teach is
+2 touch a life
4 ever

2 teach is
+2 touch a life
4 ever

Grades

Teacher Magnet & Pencil Holder

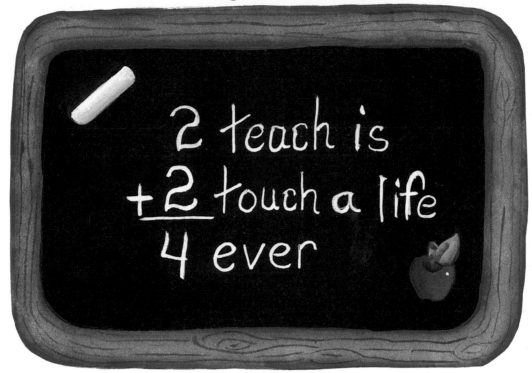

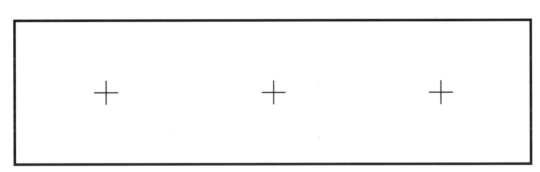

Pencil Holder Diagram (top view)

Materials if for magnet:
1/4" Baltic birch plywood
All purpose glue
Paint (coordinated colors)
Magnetic strips

Instructions if for magnet:
Adhere color copy to plywood. Cut out design. Paint the back and edges of the work piece. Glue magnet strips to the back of work piece.

Materials if for pencil holder:
1 1/2" X 5 3/8" wood of choice
Paint (coordinated colors)
Pencils or Pens of choice

Instructions if for pencil holder:
Adhere color copy to wood. Cut out design. Drill three holes 1 1/2" deep in top of work piece to accommodate the pencils or pens. *See Pencil Holder Diagram.* Paint the back and edges of the work piece.

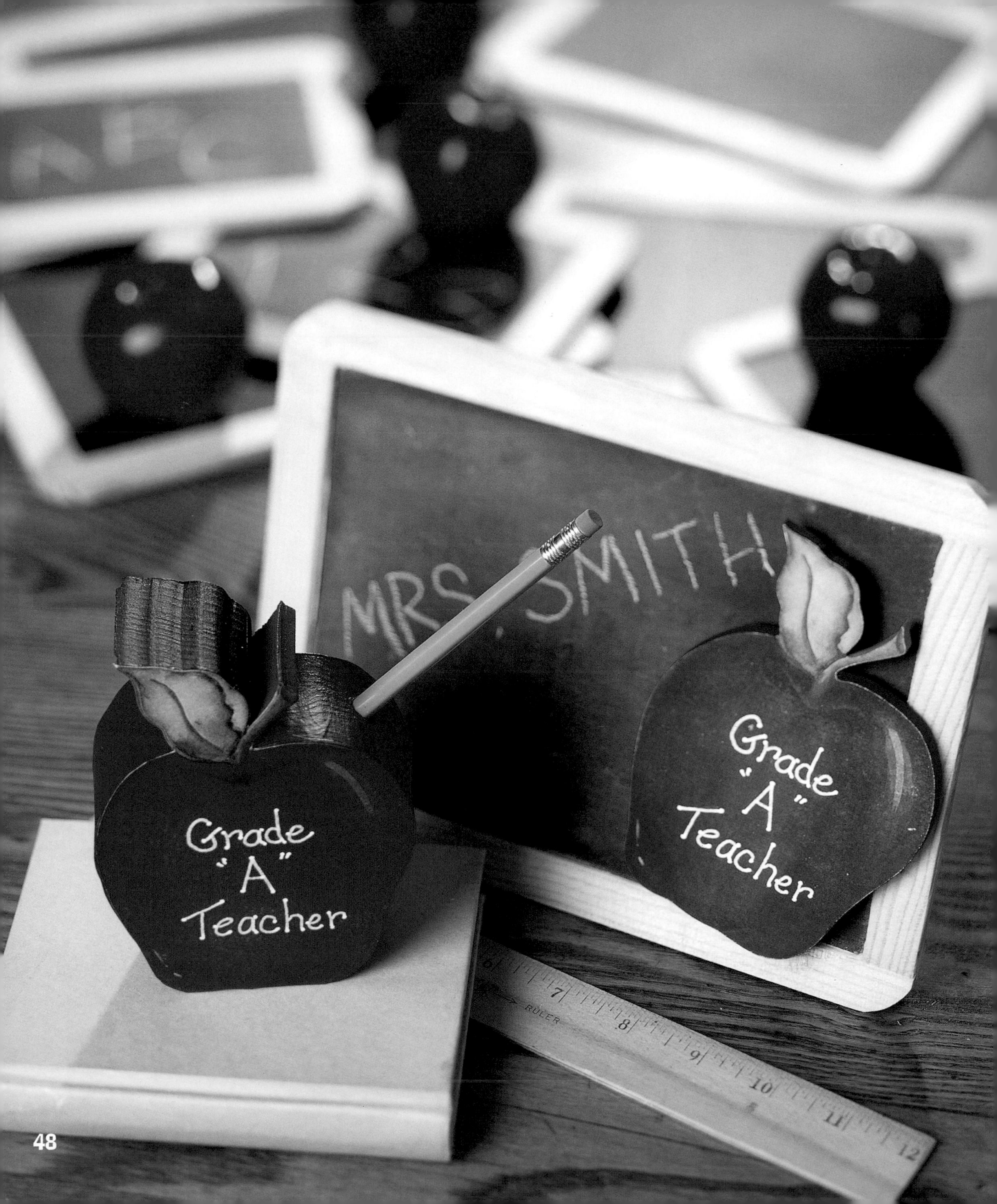
MRS. SMITH
Grade
"A"
Teacher
Grade
"A"
Teacher

Apple Magnet & Pencil Holder

Materials if for magnet:
1/4" Baltic birch plywood
All purpose glue
Paint (coordinated colors)
Magnetic strips

Instructions if for magnet:
Adhere color copy to plywood. Cut out design.
Paint the back and edges of the work piece.
Glue magnetic strips to the back of work piece.

Materials if for pencil holder:
1 1/2" wood of choice
Paint (coordinated colors)
Pencil or pen of choice

Instructions if for pencil holder:
Adhere color copy to wood. Cut out design. Drill
hole into the upper right side of the work piece
1 1/2" deep to accommodate the pencil or pen.
Paint the back and edges of the work piece.

What I Did at School Today

Materials if for magnet:
1/4" Baltic birch plywood
All purpose glue
Paint (coordinated colors)
Magnetic strips
Small clothespins (2)
Black permanent marker

Materials if for hanging work piece:
1/4" Baltic birch plywood
All purpose glue
Paint (coordinated colors)
Picture frame hanger
Small clothespins (2)
Black permanent marker

Instructions if for magnet:
Adhere color copy to plywood. Cut out design. Paint the back and edges of the work piece. Glue magnetic strips to back of work piece. Glue small clothespins to each side of base. *See photo on opposite page.* Using a black permanent marker, personalize the sign above the door.

Instructions if for hanging work piece:
Adhere color copy to plywood. Cut out design. Paint the back and edges of the work piece. Attach picture frame hanger to back of work piece. Glue small clothespins to each side of base. *See photo on opposite page.* Using a black permanent marker, personalize the sign above the door.

Pansy Butterfly

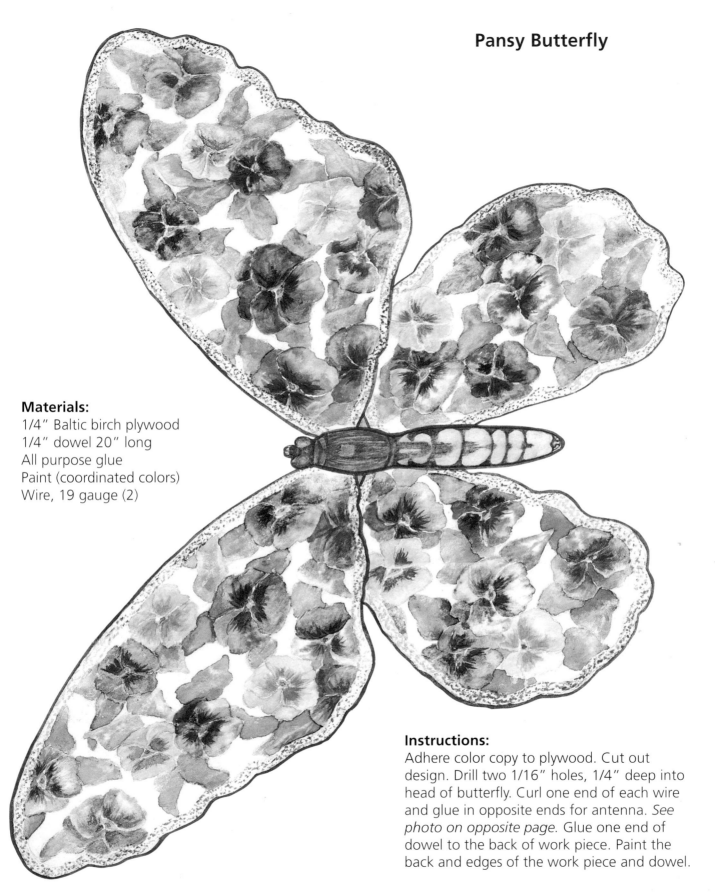

Materials:
1/4" Baltic birch plywood
1/4" dowel 20" long
All purpose glue
Paint (coordinated colors)
Wire, 19 gauge (2)

Instructions:
Adhere color copy to plywood. Cut out design. Drill two 1/16" holes, 1/4" deep into head of butterfly. Curl one end of each wire and glue in opposite ends for antenna. *See photo on opposite page.* Glue one end of dowel to the back of work piece. Paint the back and edges of the work piece and dowel.

Birdhouse Key Holder

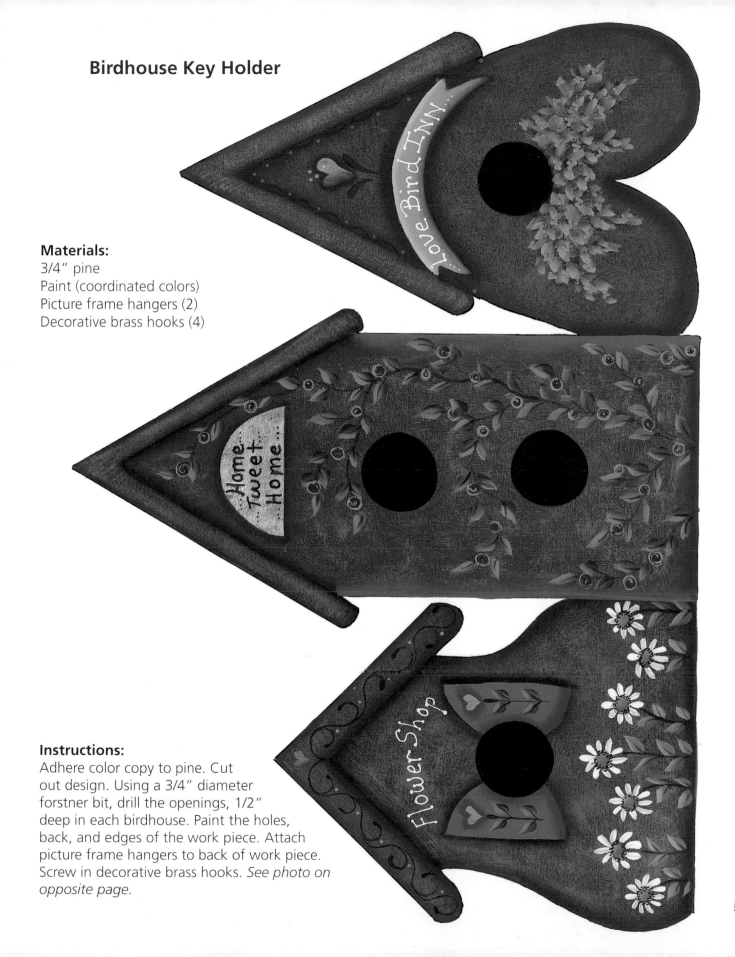

Materials:
3/4" pine
Paint (coordinated colors)
Picture frame hangers (2)
Decorative brass hooks (4)

Instructions:
Adhere color copy to pine. Cut out design. Using a 3/4" diameter forstner bit, drill the openings, 1/2" deep in each birdhouse. Paint the holes, back, and edges of the work piece. Attach picture frame hangers to back of work piece. Screw in decorative brass hooks. *See photo on opposite page.*

A Key House

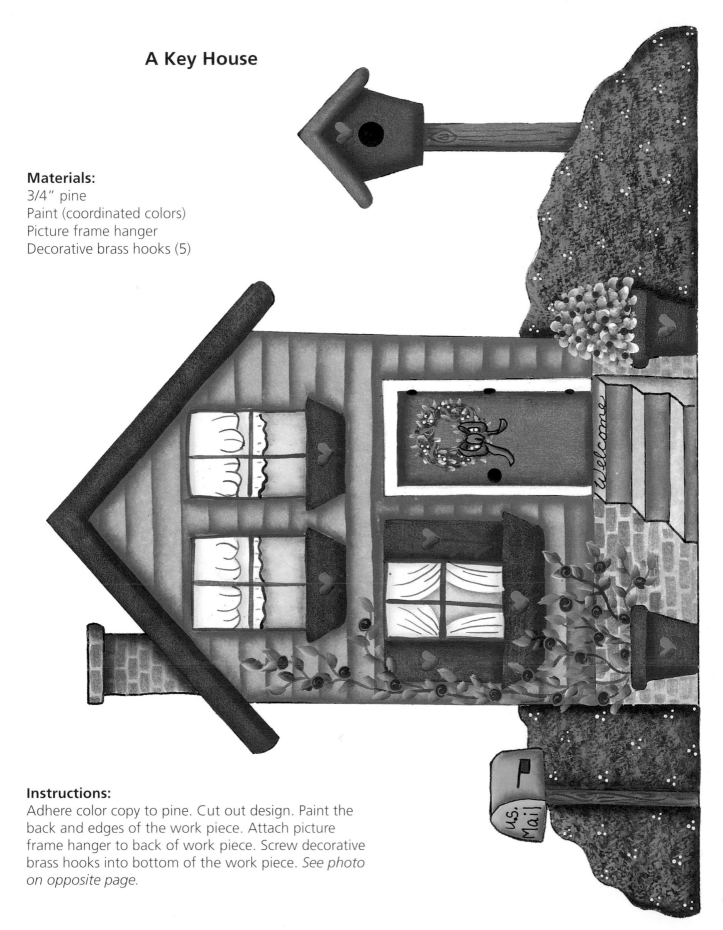

Materials:
3/4" pine
Paint (coordinated colors)
Picture frame hanger
Decorative brass hooks (5)

Instructions:
Adhere color copy to pine. Cut out design. Paint the back and edges of the work piece. Attach picture frame hanger to back of work piece. Screw decorative brass hooks into bottom of the work piece. *See photo on opposite page.*

Birdhouse Clock

Materials:
3/4" pine
1/4" dowel 12" long
All purpose glue
Paint (coordinated colors)
Oval clock works
Moss (optional)
Greenery (optional)
Flowers (optional)
Fence (optional)

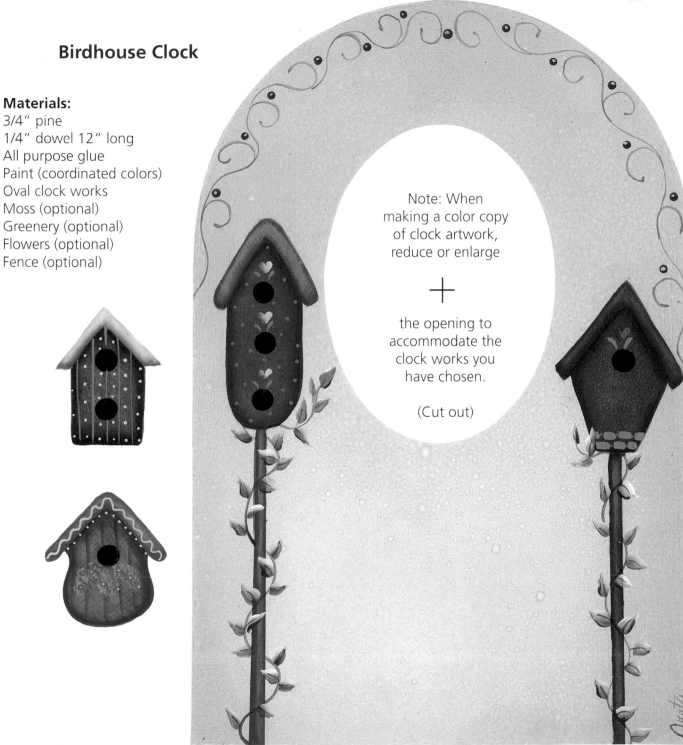

Note: When making a color copy of clock artwork, reduce or enlarge

$+$

the opening to accommodate the clock works you have chosen.

(Cut out)

Instructions:
Adhere color copies to pine. Cut out designs. Cut out hole to accommodate clock works. Insert clock works. Cut out a 3/4" X 2" X 7 1/2" base from pine. Drill two 1/4" holes, 1/2" deep for placement of birdhouses. *See photo on opposite page.* Center and glue the bottom of the work piece even with the back edge of the base. Cut 1/4" dowel into two desired lengths. Drill 1/4" holes, 1/2" deep into the bottoms of the birdhouses, and glue in dowels. Glue remaining ends of dowels into base. Paint the back and edges of the work piece. Paint base as desired. Add moss, greenery, flowers, and fence (optional).

Laundry Line

Materials:
1/4" Baltic birch plywood
3/4" pine
1/4" dowel 8" long (2)
All purpose glue
Paint (coordinated colors)
1/2"-diameter wooden beads (2) (optional)
Twine, 2 ply
Mini clothespins (9)

Instructions:
Adhere color copies for clothing to plywood. Cut out designs. Adhere color copy for basket to pine. Cut out design. Cut out a 3/4" X 2" X 11 1/2" base from pine. Round off edges of base if desired. Paint the backs and edges of the work pieces. Sand down one end of each 1/4" dowel to fit in a 1/2"-diameter wooden bead. Glue one bead to one end of each dowel. Drill one 1/4" hole, 1/2" deep at each end of the base. Glue in remaining ends of the dowels. Glue basket to the base. *See photo on opposite page.* Paint the base and dowels. Tie twine to each dowel near bead. Attach clothing to the twine with clothespins.

Night, Night Bear

Materials:
1/4" Baltic birch plywood
Paint (coordinated colors)
Picture frame hanger
Decorative brass hook

Instructions:
Adhere color copy to plywood.
Cut out design. Paint the back and
edges of the work piece. Attach
picture frame hanger to back of
work piece. Screw in decorative
brass hook. *See photo on opposite
page.*

Materials:
1/4" Baltic birch plywood
3/4" wood of choice
All purpose glue
Paint or stain (coordinated colors)
Picture frame hangers (2)

Instructions:
Adhere color copies of letters to plywood. Cut out designs. Paint the backs and edges of the work pieces. Evenly lay out letters of name or wording as desired to determine the length of the plaque/backer. Cut out a 1 3/4" X required length plaque/backer from wood of choice for mounting the letters on. Evenly space and glue letters to plaque/backer. Paint or stain edges and face of plaque/backer. Attach picture frame hangers to back of plaque/backer on each end.

Bunny Board

Materials:
1/4" Baltic birch plywood
All purpose glue
Paint (coordinated colors)
Cork board with frame (purchased)
Picture frame hanger

Instructions:
Adhere color copies to plywood. Cut out designs.
Paint the backs and edges of the work pieces.
Attach picture frame hanger to the back of the
cork board frame. Glue pieces to the cork board
frame. *See photo on opposite page.*

Floral Clock

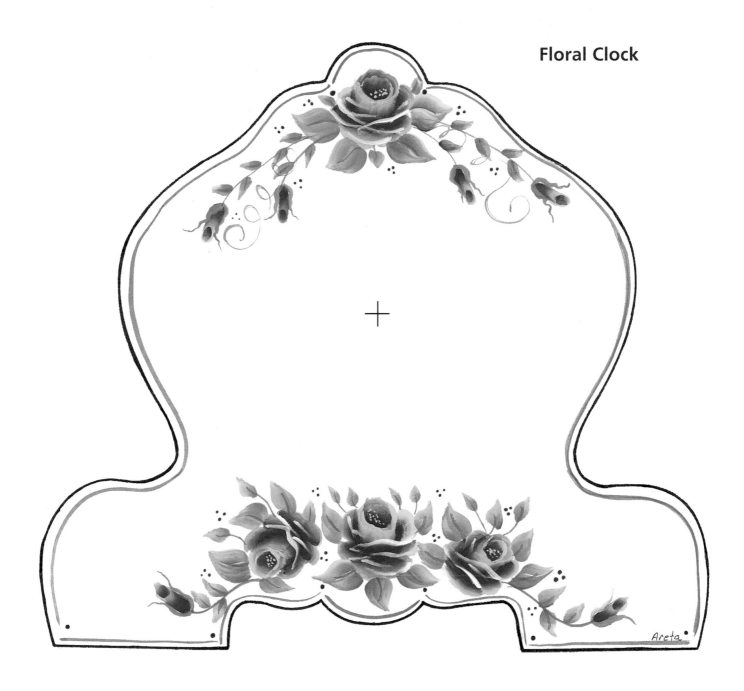

Materials:
1 1/2" wood of choice
Paint (coordinated colors)
Clock works
Felt pads or rubber feet

Instructions:
Adhere color copy to wood. Cut out design.
Layout opening for clock works. Cut or drill out
hole to accommodate clock works. Insert clock
works. Paint the back and edges of the work
piece. Attach felt pads or rubber feet to base of
work piece.

Materials:
1/4" Baltic birch plywood
All purpose glue
Paint (coordinated colors)
Magnetic strips

Instructions:
Adhere color copies to plywood. Cut out designs. Paint the backs and edges of the work pieces. Glue magnetic strips to backs of work pieces.

Note: When making a color copy of clock artwork, reduce or enlarge the opening to accommodate the clock works you have chosen.

Materials:
3/4" pine
Paint (coordinated colors)
Clock works

Instructions:
Adhere color copy to pine. Cut out design. Cut or drill out hole to accommodate clock works. Insert clock works. Paint the back and edges of the work piece.

Bear & Hearts

Materials:
3/4" pine
Paint (coordinated colors)

Instructions:
Adhere color copy to pine. Cut out design. Paint the back and edges of the work piece.

Scrapbook Cover

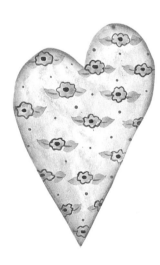

Materials:
1/4" Baltic birch plywood
1/8" Baltic birch plywood
All purpose glue
Paint (coordinated colors)
Scrapbook album

Instructions:
Adhere color copy for base to 1/4" plywood. Cut out design. Adhere color copies for hearts to 1/8" plywood. Cut out designs. Paint the back and edges of the work pieces. Glue hearts onto front of the scrapbook work piece. Glue finished work piece to the cover of a scrapbook album.

Halloween Trio

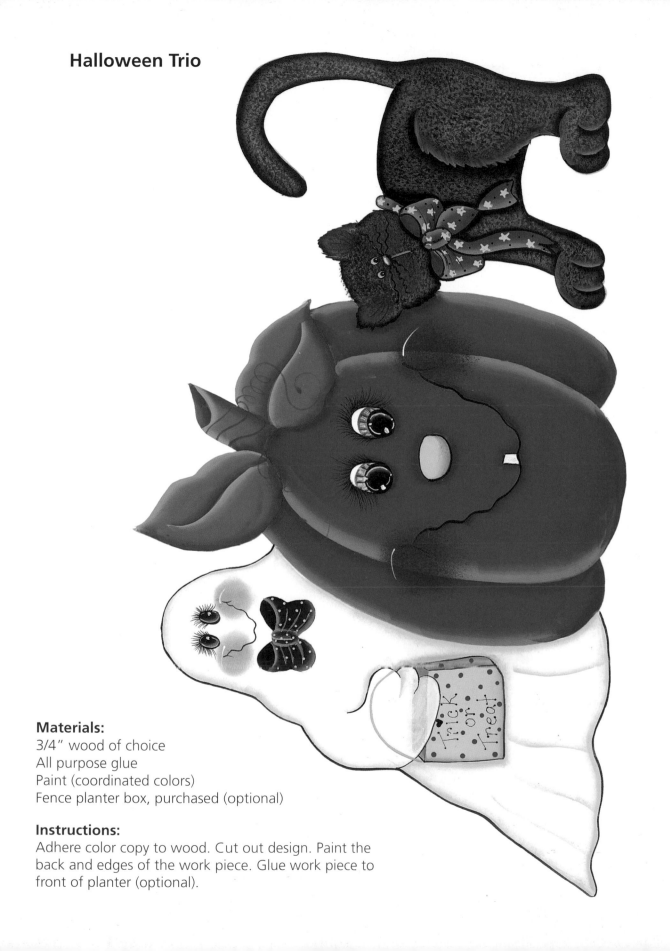

Materials:
3/4" wood of choice
All purpose glue
Paint (coordinated colors)
Fence planter box, purchased (optional)

Instructions:
Adhere color copy to wood. Cut out design. Paint the
back and edges of the work piece. Glue work piece to
front of planter (optional).

Gargoyle

Materials:
3/4" pine
Paint (coordinated colors)
Small eye screws (2)
Length of chain

Instructions:
Adhere color copy to pine. Cut out design.
Paint the back and edges of the work piece.
Screw in eyescrews to top edge of each wing.
Cut chain to desired length. Attach chain to
eyescrews.

Light Switch Covers

Materials:
1/8" Baltic birch plywood
Paint (coordinated colors)

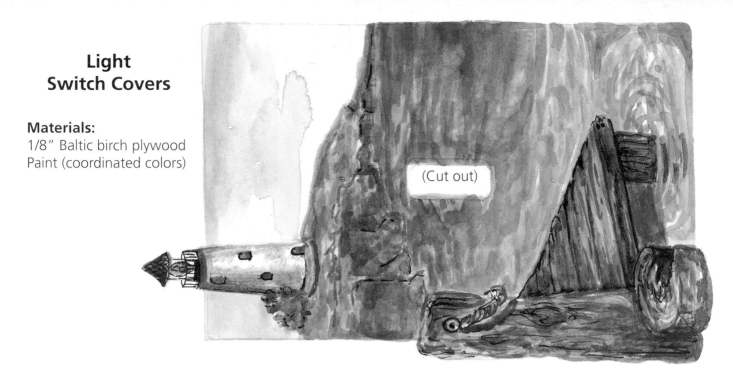

(Cut out)

Note: When making copies of this artwork, make certain that the opening for the light switch is the required size to fit the light switch that is to be covered.

(Cut out)

Instructions:
Adhere color copies to plywood. Cut out designs. Paint edges of each work piece. Measure screw holes on outlet, mark, and drill them in each work piece.

Seasonal Tree & Ornaments

Note: There are five sets of six ornaments provided for this project so you can change them with the seasons and holidays throughout the year. Celebrate Valentine's day *(See below and pages 91–92)*, the birth of a baby *(See page 93)*, Halloween *(See pages 94–96)*, the arrival of autumn *(See pages 96–97)*, and finally Christmas *(See page 98)*. There are also three extra hearts that you can choose from for the tree topper *(See below and pages 91–92)*.

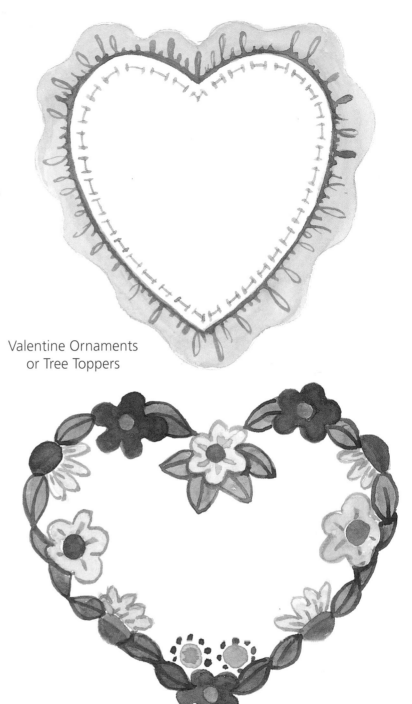

Valentine Ornaments
or Tree Toppers

Materials:
3/4″ wood of choice
  (hanging figures of choice)
Paint (coordinated colors)
Figure tree, purchased or refer
  to Materials and Instructions for
  tree assembly on page 90
Small eye screws (6)
Raffia (optional)

Instructions:
Adhere color copies for seven figures (one should be a heart for topper) to wood. Cut out designs. Paint and embellish the backs and edges of the work pieces. Drill a 3/8″ hole, 1/2″ deep into the bottom of the topper. Set topper onto dowel on top of figure tree. Screw small eye screws into the tops of the remaining work pieces. Tie on raffia (optional). Hang work pieces on cup hooks on figure tree as desired.

Materials for tree assembly:

3/4" wood of choice (base)
1 1/2" X 1 1/2" X 16" wood
   of choice (center post)
3/8" dowels 5 1/2" long (6)
3/8" dowel 1" long (1)
All purpose glue
Paint (coordinated colors)
1 1/2" wood screw (1)
Small cup hooks (6)

Instructions for tree assembly:

•Shape top of 1 1/2" X 1 1/2" X
16" wood (center post). Drill three
3/8" holes, 1/2" deep on each
side of the center post. *See Figure
Tree Diagram*.

•Glue 5 1/2" dowels into the six
holes. Drill a 3/8" hole, 1/2" deep
into the top of the center post.
Glue 1" dowel into top of center
post.

•Cut out 3/4" X 4" X 6" base
from wood of choice. Drill 1/8"
hole through center line. Sand
base. Center the post onto the
base and attach with the wood
screw through the bottom of the
base.

•Paint figure tree. Screw small cup
hooks into the center bottom of
each dowel.

Figure Tree Diagram

1 1/2"

5"

5"

5"

16"

Center Post
(Center line)

Base
4" x 6"

(Center line)

Valentine Ornaments
or Tree Toppers

Valentine Ornaments
or Tree Toppers

Baby Ornaments

93

Halloween Ornaments

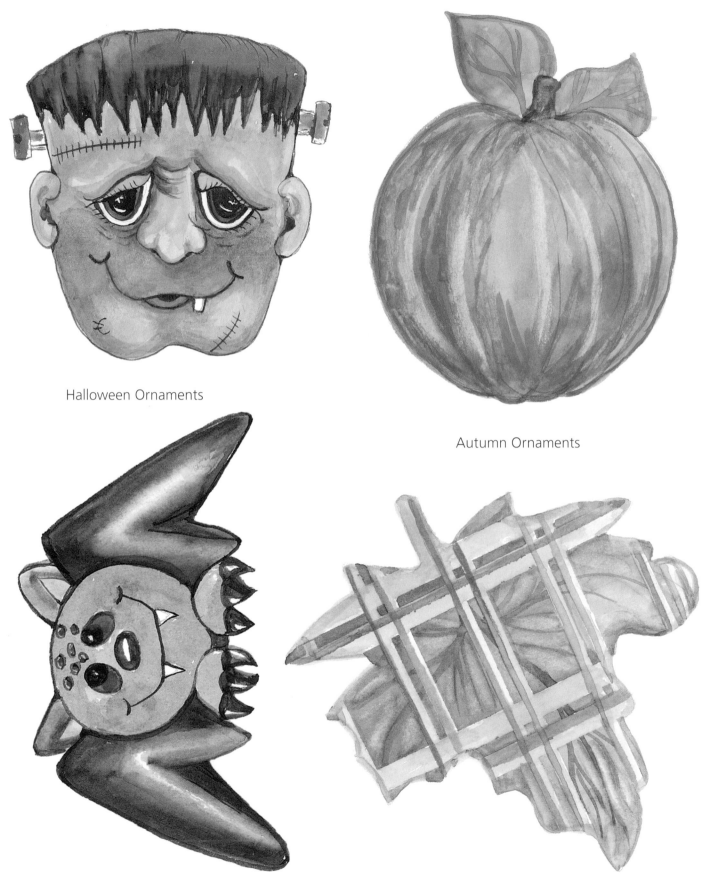

Halloween Ornaments

Autumn Ornaments

Autumn Ornaments

Christmas Ornaments

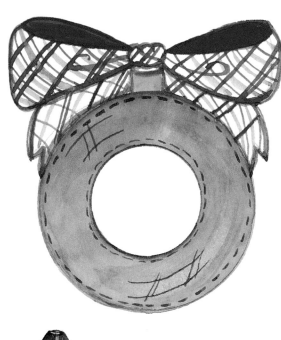

Garland Ornaments

Materials:
1/4" Baltic birch plywood
All purpose glue
Paint (coordinated colors)
Decorative wire,
   24 guage
Garland (purchased)

Instructions:
Adhere color copies
to plywood. Cut out
designs. Paint the backs
and edges of the work
pieces. Glue wings to
back of girl. Glue holly
to front of Santa.
Drill 1/16" holes
through each work
piece and attach wire.
Attach wired work
pieces to garland as
desired.

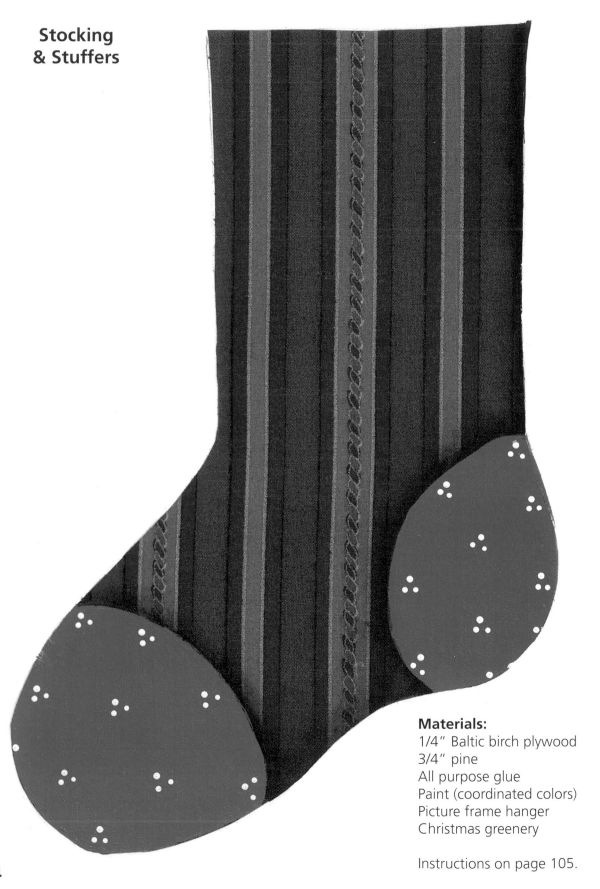

Materials:
1/4" Baltic birch plywood
3/4" pine
All purpose glue
Paint (coordinated colors)
Picture frame hanger
Christmas greenery

Instructions on page 105.

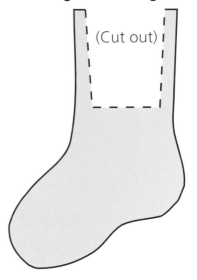

Stocking Pocket Diagram

(Cut out)

Materials on page 104.

Instructions:
Adhere color copy for stocking to plywood. Nail workpiece to pine and a second piece of blank plywood. Cut all three pieces together. Cut out an opening in the top section of the pine sock to create a pocket. *See Stocking Pocket Diagram.* Glue the aligned stocking pieces together with the pine sandwiched between the work piece and plywood for back. Sand edges. Paint back and edges of the work piece. Adhere color copies for stocking cuff and gifts to plywood. Cut out designs. Paint backs and edges of the work pieces. Glue cuff in place. *See photo on opposite page.* Attach picture frame hanger to back. Insert Christmas greenery and gifts into pocket.

Better Not Pout

Materials:
3/4" pine
1/4" Baltic birch plywood
All purpose glue
Paint (coordinated colors)

Instructions:
Adhere color copy of Santa to pine. Cut out design. Adhere color copy of banner to plywood. Cut out design. Paint the back and edges of the work pieces. Glue banner to front of Santa, aligning hands to arms.

A Snowman Family

Materials:
3/4" wood of choice
1/4" Baltic birch plywood
All purpose glue
Paint (coordinated colors)
Twigs

Instructions:
Adhere color copies of snowpeople to wood of choice. Cut out designs. Adhere color copies of scarf and tie *(See page 110)* to plywood. Cut out designs. Paint backs and edges of the work pieces. Glue tie and scarf to snowmen. *See photo on opposite page.* Drill holes, 1/2" deep into side edges of each snowperson to accommodate twigs for arms. Glue in twigs.

Animal Ornaments

Materials:
1/4" Baltic birch plywood
Paint (coordinated colors)
Decorative string

Instructions:
Adhere color copies to plywood. Cut out designs. Paint back and edges of the work pieces. Drill 1/16" hole through the top of each work piece. Tie on a length of decorative string for hanger.

Joy Wall Hanger

(Cut out)

Materials:
3/4" wood of choice
All purpose glue
Paint (coordinated colors)
Small eye screws (4)
Picture frame hanger
Raffia
Christmas greenery
Wire,19 gauge
Bells (2)

Instructions:
Adhere color copy to wood. Cut out design. Paint back and edges of the work piece. Screw eye screws into the bottom edges of the letters, placing one on the bottom of both the "I" and "Y" and two slightly apart on the bottom of the "O." Attach picture frame hanger to back of work piece. Tie raffia into a bow and attach Christmas greenery to raffia bow with wire. Wire completed raffia bow and greenery to work piece through the eye screws. Tie bells with hanging raffia at varied heights. *See photo on opposite page.*

All Warm and Wooly

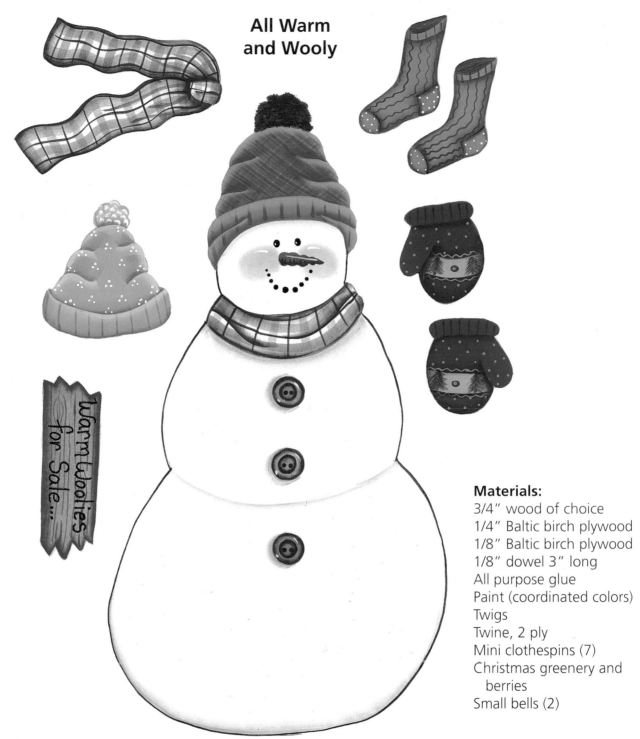

Materials:
3/4" wood of choice
1/4" Baltic birch plywood
1/8" Baltic birch plywood
1/8" dowel 3" long
All purpose glue
Paint (coordinated colors)
Twigs
Twine, 2 ply
Mini clothespins (7)
Christmas greenery and
   berries
Small bells (2)

Instructions:
Adhere color copy for snowman body to wood of choice. Cut out snowman. Paint the back and edges of the work piece. Drill holes 1/2" deep in side edges of snowman to accommodate twigs for arms. Glue in twigs. Adhere color copies for sign and scarf to 1/4" plywood. Cut out designs. Drill a 1/8" hole from top to bottom through the sign. Glue in 1/8" dowel. Adhere color copies for clothing pieces to 1/8" plywood. Cut out designs. Paint backs and edges of the work pieces. Cut out 1 1/2" X 6" base from wood of choice. Paint base as desired. Drill 1/8" hole, 1/2" deep into base. Glue in sign. Glue scarf to snowman. Glue snowman to center of base. Attach clothing pieces to twine with mini clothes pins. Tie twine with clothing to twig arms. *See photo on opposite page.* Attach Christmas greenery with mini clothespins. Glue on berries and bells.

Santa Greeting Card Holder

Materials list and instructions on page 120.

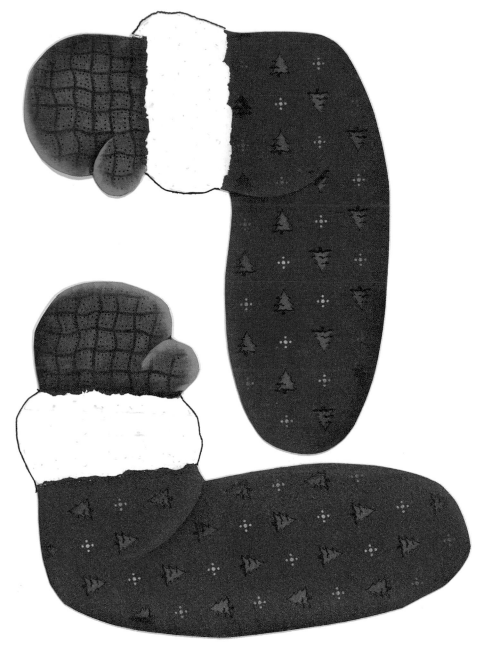

Materials:
3/4" wood of choice
1/4" Baltic birch plywood
All purpose glue
Paint (coordinated colors)
Box, purchased or refer to
  Materials and Instructions for
  box assembly on opposite page
Decorative wire, 24 gauge
Bell

Instructions:
Adhere color copy for Santa body to wood of choice. Cut out design. Drill small hole through Santa's hat. Adhere color copies for Santa arms to plywood. Cut out designs. Paint backs and edges of work pieces. Paint purchased or assembled box. Glue Santa and arms to box. *See photo on page 118.* Attach the bell with the decorative wire. Using scissors, cut out and adhere color copy for "Greetings" to front of box.

Box Diagram 1

Front and Back

End

1/4" X 5" X 5"
(box bottom)

Box Diagram 2

1/4" X 4" X 5 1/2 " (ends)   1/4" X 4" X 5" (front and back)

Materials for box assembly:
1/4" X 4" X 5" pine
   (front and back – 2)
1/4" X 4" X 5 1/2" pine (ends – 2)
1/4" X 5" X 5" pine (box bottom)
All purpose glue

Instructions for box assembly:
Set box bottom on a flat surface and glue box front, back, and sides together around the box bottom.
See Box Diagrams 1 and 2.

Materials:
1 1/2" wood of choice
1/8" dowel 2" long (3)
All purpose glue
Paint (coordinated colors)

Instructions:
Adhere color copies to wood, separating the stars from the trees. Cut out designs. Drill 1/8" hole 1/4" deep into both the top of the trees and the bottom of the stars. Paint backs and edges of the work pieces and the dowels. Glue in the dowels to the base of the stars. Glue in the remainig end of the dowels to the top of the trees.

Three Christmas Trees

124

INCHES TO MILLIMETRES AND CENTIMETRES

MM-Millimetres   CM-Centimetres

INCHES	MM	CM	INCHES	CM	INCHES	CM
1/8	3	0.9	9	22.9	30	76.2
1/4	6	0.6	10	25.4	31	78.7
3/8	10	1.0	11	27.9	32	81.3
1/2	13	1.3	12	30.5	33	83.8
5/8	16	1.6	13	33.0	34	86.4
3/4	19	1.9	14	35.6	35	88.9
7/8	22	2.2	15	38.1	36	91.4
1	25	2.5	16	40.6	37	94.0
1 1/4	32	3.2	17	43.2	38	96.5
1 1/2	38	3.8	18	45.7	39	99.1
1 3/4	44	4.4	19	48.3	40	101.6
2	51	5.1	20	50.8	41	104.1
2 1/2	64	6.4	21	53.3	42	106.7
3	76	7.6	22	55.9	43	109.2
3 1/2	89	8.9	23	58.4	44	111.8
4	102	10.2	24	61.0	45	114.3
4 1/2	114	11.4	25	63.5	46	116.8
5	127	12.7	26	66.0	47	119.4
6	152	15.2	27	68.6	48	121.9
7	178	17.8	28	71.1	49	124.5
8	203	20.3	29	73.7	50	127.0

Index: